JUST LIVING,
LOVING AND
CARING

JUST LIVING, LOVING AND CARING

AUNT NETTE

Rev. date: 08/16/2013

To order additional copies of this book, contact:
Xlibris LLC
1-888-795-4274
www.Xlibris.com
Orders@Xlibris.com
74097

Contents

SECTION III—Epilogue: Collection of Personal Treasures Reflecting Living, Loving and Caring

About the Author

Dr. Marionette Sanders Daniels
Silver Spring MD, 20910

Pen Name; Aunt Nette. *Born*: Union, South Carolina—the oldest of three children (two boys) of the Late William and Essie Moorehead Sanders. *Married:* Edward Daniels of Louisa, Virginia. *Education:* West Virginia State College and Columbia University School of Social Work. *Occupation*: Social Work Consultant and Health Educator. *Faith:* Baptist—*Member*—St. Mary's Baptist Church, Washington, DC.

Marionette Sanders Daniels, fondly known as "Aunt Nette", first began writing poetry in the mid-1970s. One of the very first was titled "Ode to My Friend." It tells the story of her interactions with a man who lived on the street outside her home in New York City, and engages an exploration into the perceived differences among people. This theme has continued throughout Daniels poetry, as she seeks to take the reader on a journey of reflection on human interactions.

Her late father was a writer who enjoyed and wrote poetry. He spent a lot of time on writing and gathering old things about the city of Union, S.C. He, at one time, had 65 or 70 pages which he hoped to have published.

As a professionally trained social worker, Marionette Sanders Daniels life's work has focused on the study and of human interactions. She completed high school in Union, South Carolina and received her undergraduate degree from West Virginia State College followed by a graduate degree at Columbia University. She is a licensed social work practitioner with experience as a mental health specialist, teacher, lecturer, author, and administrator. She served as Director of the Methodone Maintenance Program at White Plains N.Y. Hospital; Social Work Supervisor of the Department of Psychiatry, Harlem Hospital, NYC; Assistant Director, Ambulatory Care and Community Outreach, Mount Sinai Medical Center; N.Y.C., Instructor and Coordinator of Community Program Planning, Mount Sinai School of Medicine NYC; Instructor and

Curriculum Developer, The New School of Social Research NYC; Field Instructor; Columbia University School of Public Health; Field Instructor, Columbia University, Hunter College, and Howard University Schools of Social Work.

She moved to Washington, D.C. in 1980 and continued her work in the field of social work as Project Coordinator, for the National Professional Child Abuse and Neglect Resource Center; Community-based Program Evaluator, Maryland State Department of Mental Health; Continuing Education Consultant, National Association of Social Workers; Special Project Consultant, Washington, DC Urban League; Health Education Consultant and Project Director of a Alzheimer's Weekend Respite Program for Family and Child Services, Inc. of Washington, DC.

She is widowed (late husband, Edward Daniels) and currently lives in an assisted living facility in Silver Spring, Maryland. She has written and published professionally and has been cited in both Who's Who of American Women and Who's Who of Women of the World.

With this book of poetry, she, (Aunt Nette), invites readers into her life experiences with the hope that they will see how one can always find some beauty at any level of human interaction. In her words, "I hope that readers will see through my poetry that we're all on God's earth together and moments of interaction between any of us is a blessing wherein lies an opportunity to express love and caring qualities."

Aunt, Nette, who are you to be writing poems?

I am
A child and follower of Jesus Christ
My poems are reflective of people to people
actions, reactions and interactions.
I have long experienced and observed the joys,
the challenges, the love, the sorrows
and the nuances of life.
My emphasis is on people to people relationships
highlighting the impact of responsive tenderness,
and love upon the life of one human being to another,
all in the name of Jesus Christ and
under the watchful eye of God Almighty, our creator.
I entered the garden of life alone, oh so very early
one morning (or so I'm told).
My memory holds no aloneness.
Always people in the garden with their space and I with mine.
Oh! There was the shoving, the pushing, the learning
the running, the falling, the leaning, the singing,
the laughing, the crying, the praying, all such going-ons
with my parents and two brothers.
Most memorable was the loving and being loved
under the watchful eye of Him who placed me in the garden of life.

Dedication

This book is dedicated to so many wonderful people who have played an important role in my life.

First, to my late husband, Edward Daniels, the man with whom I was blessed to share a marriage and a mutual passion under the watchful eye of God for 60 years.

Secondly, to my late father and mother, William and Essie Moorehead Sanders and my two brothers the late Rev. James W. Sanders, Sr. and the late Deacon Grady M. Sanders, Sr.

Thirdly, it is dedicated to my sisters-in-law, Rubye Corry Sanders, Lillie M. Wigfall Sanders, Adele Daniels Johnson, and the late Margaret Lovelace.

Next, it is dedicated to my nieces, nephews and God-children to whom I owe both love and thanks for precious memories: Jewette (Roger) Patterson, Ruzlin (Leroy) Smith, Rev. James W. Sanders, Jr., Rev. Grady M. (Cherette) Sanders, Jr., the late Pamela W. Redfearn, Rev. Charles W. (Theresa) Sanders, Sr., Marionette E. Nyako, the late Stephanie Cuthbertson, Mattie S. Davis, Raiford J. Sanders, Marshall (Lorette) Hackney, Arthur (Jacqueline) Hackney, Katrina Williams, Gail Christmas, Inga B. (Clifton) Mason, Samantha Butts, Gregory (Emma) Anderson, Eddie (Charlesette) Clark, Jerry Christian, Jennie (Mark) Harvey, Dave (Grace) Poland and Renee Perry.

In addition, I am truly indebted to the precious souls, friends and relatives alike, who have inspired and encouraged me over the years. Among them I must mention: Dr. Helaine Daniels, Attorney & Mrs. Derrick Humphries, Rev. and Mrs. Darryl (Joan) Crump, Ms. Jonah Humphries, Dr. Stacy Nicholson, Dr. Hilda Richards, Terria McAllister, Derrick McAllister, Brenda Alford and Noel Ali Muller.

To all of these people, plus others whose names are regretfully not included here I am indebted to and thank God for the inspiration and support they have provided thru the years.

Section I

Togetherness In Life's Garden

Gathering

Like the careful selection of seeds and buds
for the next planting season,
So I will select and gather treasures from life.
I'll take each shared tender moment of togetherness,
Wrap it carefully in the finest of memory tissue
Guard it jealously for use in the coming years.
When I'm alone with thoughts of you my memory
wrapped treasures, like loving friends,
will sprout forth for me to enjoy.

Know You?

Know you?
Let me see-
On a busy day in a crowded store,
I look up
across two counters, your eyes in a smiling
face send a happy "Hello".
My eyes send a delighted "Hello" in response.
Forget you and the joy of a special moment?
Never!
Know you? Oh yes, you are a people
whose spirit for a moment connected with mine.

People to People

The garden variety type?
People with a bit of "this" and "that"?
People nurtured only by nature?
Who but God really knows the "this" and "that" of you or of me?

Necessities of Life: For the Garden—For the People

For the garden—Sunshine
For people—Laughter
For the garden—Water
For people—Tears
For the garden—a Spade
For people—a Touch
For the garden—a Fence
For people—Understanding
For both—Love

This poem was the outgrowth of a moment shared with my mother who one day spoke of the joy of seeing the sunshine on her garden following a deluge of rain.

Does it Matter?

Does it matter what we do in service for others?
Before we answer,
consider that a smile, a hello, and a thank you
makes any encounter worthwhile.

Room to Bloom

Make room for you to bloom
Why not?
Here we are, so near each other, yet
each of us in our very own spot.
We grow, we blossom at our own pace.
Your blossoming out,
gently touches and steadily moves me aside
Remember, it was you
permitting me to lean on you that was the strength beneath my last
blossom.
Not you?
Does it really matter my friend?
I am here strong at the moment.
Lean on me.
Grow and blossom.
Your beauty enhances me until I can bloom again.

People

P is for the patience people need from each other.
E is for the effort people must make to others.
O is for the openness to seek out and find the good in others.
P is for pleasure found in the warmth of people relationships.
L is for the love as commanded by God for Him and all
who reside in life's garden.
E is for the eagerness to seek out other people and to please our God

Section II

Simply Life Encounters

An Ode to My Friend of the West 98th Street Transient House,

Part I
I see you—Do you see me?

I see you—I greet you
Here I lean, morning, noon and evening, always with
one shoulder touching the column
Can't you see the difference between the column and me?
Can't you really tell where I begin and end?
Can't you tell what part is column and what part is me, a people?
Can't you say hello to me? I'm a people . . .

Ode Pt. II
Growing Buds of Friendship

Passing by you made me grow—But how was I to know
I could so easily have missed a golden opportunity to grow!
Surely, you know how you must have looked—your dirty,
disheveled appearance-
Your thick, hoarse-sounding voice forcing its way through
A whiskey laden, weary throat.
But there you were, day-in and day-out, offering a quick courteous nod
As a "Good Morning" and "Good Evening" was heard
From the same weary-sounding throat near the same door stoop.
My response was so automatic but the
twinkle in your eyes kept my response to you
Wrapped in a cautious bud of friendliness.
Is there any wonder I didn't know you, reclining
comfortably on the park bench?
Do you know why I had to stop and take a hard look
when a familiar voice
Accompanied by a hearty laugh asks, "Don't you know me?"
Know you? A smiling person, sitting straight, wearing clean,
well-pressed pants and
a clean shirt—Know you? With clear eyes dancing mischievously,
And a head held high?
No, I don't think—Wait a minute! Another time a
few months ago, there was another
you!
One from whom I accepted and responded to a continuing
morning and afternoon greeting.
I never ceased to be amazed by your constant vigil, just resting
In that same ole spot twice a day.
How nice to see what surely must be the real you!
Hello, my neighbor and my friend!

Ode Pt. III
Here Today, Tomorrow Gone

My! I am glad to see you now remembering how I first reacted
to your morning and evening greetings.
Here we are, so many months later and I have to ask your name
when I want my parents to meet you.
You, so regal in your manner, showing so much warmth and
loving regards as you bow to them.
Is there any wonder they felt special and later asked who you were?
My friend, for weeks, now the mornings and evenings feel a bit empty.
You've gone somewhere.
Who are you? How are you? Where did you go?
I've been looking and wondering for a long time now.
But, like a precious blossom in the wild you suddenly appeared
in my life with a strange but wonderful beauty, only to
disappear just as suddenly leaving precious memories of a
brief but beautiful people to people encounter orchestrated by
a loving, caring God!

Ode Part. IV
Scattered Thoughts

I think now of my growing years
when I was taught to speak to people because it was courteous, respectful
and the thing for good people to do.
I read a saying many years later.
"If anyone is worthy of God letting them live—surely they are worthy of a
'Hello, how are you?'"
My friend must have felt the same way to stand and greet
a stranger so courteously day in and day out.
Oh! What a story about life and a precious memory.

Friendships

Part I
Friendships Do Survive

*A*lways sensitive to the mood, to the feelings and the moment.

*L*ovingly wrapped words, carefully spoken in whatever way needed.

*M*aking the most of the moment, to be cherished until the next opportunity to share.

*A*nother try and another and another, if by chance derailed, the relationship must be put back on track.

*T*rusting the mutual caring bond, there is strength, courage and love enough to survive exposure to thoughtless, selfish moments.

Part II
Letters Between Friends

Alma T:

However simple and unsophisticated, I have visions of this and my other poems being published one day. I hope you find some pleasure in this one—given the story of my surprise in discovering that the first letter of each sentence when put together spells your name.

Love,
Nette
June 16, 1993

Hi Nette!

As you can see, I really treasure some *pieces*!! This was one.
I hope it finds a place in the private pages—

Love,
Alma T.
April 18, 2008

What, if? Would I?

Oh! My dear fellow man!
What if you were a flower?
Would I lash out when you droop or seem weak?
Or, would I touch and nourish you gently?
Oh! My dear fellowman!
What if I were to treat you gently as a precious flower?

A Missed Opportunity

We meet-each walking along the same street moving in
different directions.
As people to people, our eyes meet as we approach
each other.
Even so quickly your eyes send an impish look bursting
forth with loud, unspoken words,
"Hello, I like what I see!"
My response, also noiseless, but, with facial expression
and body movement spoke just as loudly.
"How dare you approach me?"
Your eyes darkened, your wide grin became a sneer
and with no sign of gentleness you yell
"Why couldn't you appreciate and just acknowledge my
compliment to you?"
The question you asked, as you yelled over your shoulder,
was oh so appropriate and so penetrating!
If only I could have acknowledged you—
we both would have gone on our way feeling better
for having passed each other.

Riding the New York City Subway

I travel by subway day by day
Watching beautiful people rushing to and fro
I look slowly, searchingly perhaps even longingly
          from face to face—ready to offer a friendly smile
There must be someone standing or sitting who wants to
          share a nod or a smile
My eyes must certainly portray a friendly nature.
Who among you will look at me and share a
          smile—just recognizing each other as people?
Not you? Nor You?
Oh! dear people. You turn your heads so quickly—
          to stare straight ahead—to re-read the headlines
Me? I sigh—look and watch dear people riding the
          subway in New York City.

Only a Point of interest—Article from National News Service
          June 19, 1999.

NEW YORK—"A mysterious man who had been riding a New York
subway train for hours before passengers discovered his corpse Monday
has been identified as Ignacio Mendez, 37, an immigrant from Ecuador
who lived in Brooklyn, police said. Newspaper reports said Mendez
immigrated in 1989, leaving his 16-year-old daughter and 9-year-old son
behind but sending money home to them when he could.

—From news services

My Beloved

So beautiful, so handsome
So desirable even when I feel less than
half-fulfilled.
I see you through eyes veiled with love.
Did you my precious ever learn to take time
to play?
To set mutual goals with another?
To really see those close to you?
To show you care and to really accept help or
an offer from another?
I get near, ever drawn by your beckoning but,
you seems not to see me, that is . . . really see me.
When you are seemingly looking at me, do you
see my struggling? Can you look and see my suffering?
Hear my cry?
Won't you try to help me know you truly care?
You can help me you know? Or can you?
Do I need first to re-look at my own momentary
expectation and desire and see you through
eyes of my love for you?

Just Reflecting

Where is and what is the place for love?
For need? For want?
Where is the place for love when we think and talk of separation?
Yes! Yes! I need to have you seek the fullness of life in your own way.
Growing and blossoming to your fullest potential.
I want that you should live, grow, and blossom
in whatever place and with whomever other seems best suited for you.
I love you and because I do, I will separate from you physically
So that you may grow and flourish
in what is fertile soil for you.
Not just for you, but, also for my own well being and growth.
Those who see us marvel at the appearance of a
smooth, beautiful relationship, little do they
know that far from being strong and healthy at the
moment, our roots have out grown our abode.
Yes, over many years our roots have intertwined at
various levels ever so tightly.
But, not unlike healthy roots in any pot or confining space,
we respond to and eagerly seek to follow a ray of sunlight
peeking through a crack.
How will you know the fullness of what it offers unless
you free yourself and embrace it whole heartedly?
Me? Once I learn how to live free, I'll seek my ray of sunlight.
Who knows?
Your ray of sunlight might also be my ray of sunlight
as we let go and let God.

Feeling Free

Be True to myself and I'll be true to you.
To free you to be yourself frees me to be myself.
Then how come I feel so miserable having
freed myself by freeing you?
August 1978

Consider—People like flowers grow and change! True Love grows
stronger but does not change.
September 1978

Right Here—Right Now— On This Day

Mend a quarrel
Search out a forgotten friend.
Dismiss suspicion and replace it with trust.
Write a love letter.
Share some treasure.
Give a soft answer.
Encourage a youth.
Manifest your loyalty in a word or deed.
Keep a promise.
Find the time.
Forego a grudge.
Forgive an enemy.
Listen!!!
Apologize if you were wrong.
Try to understand needs of other you meet.
Examine your demands.
Think first of someone else.
Appreciate! Appreciate! Appreciate!
Be kind, be gentle.
Laugh a little more.
Deserve confidence.
Take up arms against malice.
Decry complacency.
Express gratitude.
Take pleasure in the beauty and wonder of the earth.
Worship and obey God.
Speak His and your love again, again, and again.
For where love is, there is no pain, no hurt, only love.
—Author unknown
Copied from a print on the wall of the office of Dr. Alan Rothfeld

Seasons for Visiting

Friends like blossoming flowers
Have their seasons for visiting and leaving a beautiful lingering fragrance
You, I have not seen for a while—the rotation of your visit is not yet due.
But the beauty and joy of your last visit bursts forth so clearly every now and then.

Oh! how I take care to enjoy the the fulness of each brief visit.
Memories gathered may have to last a lifetime.

Nov. 1976

Section III—Epilogue

Collection of Personal Treasures Reflecting Living, Loving and Caring

I.
Remembering

Remembering is magic!
It appears in its own time and in its own way.
What would life be like without it?
It's not important what triggers it.
If it is loving, interesting, or helpful
"relive it" with thanks to God
and a joyous heart.

II.
Edward Daniels—Expressions of Just Living, Loving, & Caring

1. Why Am I Lonely?

My Dear 'Net,

After having participated in the blessings of liberty, domestic tranquility, and the general welfare of my hotel room the entire 4th (July Holiday), I'm pleased to return to Youth House where there is a different kind of American heritage (unhappy youngsters) whose hopes and dreams and aspirations seem shattered by forces beyond their capacity to comprehend and handle.

They became restless and doubt-ridden, the results is action. Sometimes deliberate, and sometimes impulsive. Do you know what it is like to be lonely? No. You were wanted and loved and you have given it to others to me, to kids and to life. Well, if you are wondering why I should write you this kind of a letter you should re-read the first paragraph. I am a fairly successful man with many friends. Oh! I've a wife who has loved and helped in every way she could and that's saying a lot. But why am I lonely? Or why was I lonely on July 4th? Because the blessings of liberty have no meaning without people—your people—not just crowds in Central Park who know nothing of your heritage or of your dreams.

So—ok, tomorrow is another day and who knows what? Let me know about your 4th of July experiences.

You will notice that I've sent this letter in Youth House envelope. You will write me at 1221 Spofford Ave and by that time I'll let you know what I'm trying to do.

Take care of yourself and write news.

Your Boy,
Ed. D.

2.   Just A Note Speaking Love Accompanying the Flowers

When something went wrong
My heart goes out to a Lady Social Worker for I'm unlike the cynical people who just don't comprehend her warmth, charm and devotion—Beside I love her—the Social Worker with a heart

Eddie D.

3.   Recommitted to Christ Jesus—(Missive left by Ed)

My Decision to Receive
Christ As My Saviour

Confessing to God that I am a sinner, and believing that the Lord
    Jesus Christ died for my sins on the cross and was raised for my
    justification, I do now receive and confess Him as my personal
    Saviour.

Signed by Edward Daniels on   Jan. 1990

Assurance As a Believer

That if thou shalt confess with thy mouth the Lord Jesus, and shalt
    believe in thine heart that God hath raised him from the dead, thou
    shalt be saved.

—Romans 10:9

Verily, verily, I say unto you. He that heareth my word, and believeth
    on him that sent me, hath everlasting life, and shall not come into
    condemnation; but is passed from death unto life.

—John 5:24

These things have I written unto you that believe on the name of the Son
    of God; that ye may know that ye have eternal life, and that ye may
    believe on the name of the Son of God.

—I John 5:13

But these are written, that ye might believe that Jesus is the Christ, the
    Son of God; and that believing ye might have life through his name.

—John 20:31

PSALM: 37
Verses: 25 thru 38

4.   Ed Daniels' Mantra

Take kindly the counsel of the years; gracefully surrendering the things of youth.
  Nuture strength of spirit to shield you in sudden misfortunes.
    But do not distress yourself with imaginings.
      Many fears are born of fatigue and loneliness.

Beyond a wholesome discipline, be gentle with yourself.
  You are a child of the universe, no less than the tree and the stars; you have a right to be here.
    And whether or not it is clear to you, no doubt the universe is unfolding as it should.

Therefore, be at peace with God, whatever you conceive him to be, and whatever your labors and aspirations, in the noisy confusion of life keep peace with your soul.
  With all its sham drudgery and broken dreams, it is still a beautiful world.

Be careful.

Strive to be happy.

   DESIDERATA

5.   Testament—Just Life Encounters

Testament # 5 A

To Whom It May Concern:

I have known Mr. Ed Daniels both professionally and personally for the last fifteen years. My first association with Mr. Daniels was as a part of a planning team organized by the Municipal Planning Office of the District of Columbia. The purpose of this team was to provide input into the development of the Human Resources section of the District of Columbia's Comprehensive Plan. Mr. Daniels brought to the team a thorough knowledge of the planning process and a thoughtful approach to the human resources arena. He also detailed the impact that the human services initiatives had on other parts of the Comprehensive Plan. In addition, he served as the liaison between the comprehensive planning process and the Department of Human Services of the District of Columbia.

Since that time, I have been involved with Mr. Daniels in several projects ranging from business development to community service. I have also sought his advice on a number of personal issues. I have found him always to be of the highest integrity and sound judgment.

I would not hesitate to recommend him for whatever endeavors or positions that he intends to pursue. If you have any questions or need further details, please call me.

Sincerely,

Clarence E. Stukes, Director
Division of School Plant Operations

Testament # 5 B

TO WHOM IT MAY CONCERN:

More and more citizens of Montgomery County are turning their attention to the issues vital to the preservation and protection of life's prospects in Montgomery County. Mr. Ed Daniels, whom I have known for more than ten years, has demonstrated that he has more than a curious interest in what happens to those of us who live here.

In matters of crime, education, business development and health, Mr. Daniels has applied a mode of thinking essential to dealing with important dimensions of quality of life. I have often discussed questions of conflicting merits with Ed, and what I remember most is his determination to resolve an issue in terms of what was good for the greatest number among us who were also the least favored. In the long run, he felt that doing more for the victims of societal neglect would overtime be the least costly.

As a member of the Planning Board, Mr. Daniels can be expected to blend two fading characteristics in public figures these days: reconnect one's private sense of right and wrong with one's public sense of right and wrong.

For the Planning Board to select Mr. Ed Daniels for the appointment he seeks will be a recognition that he represents a mixture of economic and cultural focus extending over many years of experience. He will add a legitimacy to the Board based on his capacity to voice the feelings and concerns of people too long absent from the matters it engages.

Sincerely yours,

Franklin H. Carpenter
Montgomery County Government
Minority Procurement Officer

Testament # 5. C

May 28, 2009

Dear Mrs. Daniels:

I wanted to express my deepest sympathy at the passing of your beloved husband Edward. He will be greatly missed, but his many accomplishments and professional contributions he made in Prince George's County, and the state of Maryland will always be remembered.

Sincerely,

Senator Ulysses Currie
Senate of Maryland

Testament # 5. D

December 16, 1999

Mr. Edward Daniels
7524 Piney Branch Road
Silver Spring MD 20910

Dear Ed:

It is a pleasure to appoint you a member of the State Use Industries Management Council for the remainder of a term of three years from October 1, 1999. Your Commission has been forwarded to the Clerk of the Circuit Court in Rockville where you are to appear and take the oath of office within the next thirty days as required by law.

Please be advised that as an appointed official the Maryland Public Ethics Law applies to you. If there are employment or professional relationships or any other interests which may pose a conflict in your service on the Council, these must be disclosed prior to your appearance before the Clerk of the Circuit Court. Enclosed you will find a self-explanatory form to disclose those interests for which you may seek exemption from the automatic prohibitions of §15-502 of the Ethics Law. Notwithstanding the granting of any exemption, you will be subject to other provisions of the Ethics Law during your term of office. Should you have any questions, please contact the State Ethics Commission directly.

As we stand at the threshold of a new millennium, I am thrilled by the unlimited opportunities and significant challenges which lie ahead. We have an exciting and aggressive agenda that will position Maryland to meet and master those challenges as we move into the twenty-first century. I am pleased you are willing to serve our citizens and I am certain your contributions will improve the quality of life for Marylanders across the State. Thank you again for your commitment. We are proud to have you on our team.

Sincerely,

Parris N. Glendening
Governor

III.
Memories of Yesteryears

1. Daddy William—"What of Love?"

If You Love Someone, Tell Him.
If you love someone, tell him so
That may be the very thing he needs to know.
Whether you are twenty-two or fifty-two
You are never too old or too young to say "I love you."
Don't put off until tonight or the next day
For these words you might not be able to say.
Yes, old man death could take you away.
So let us say, "I love you," today.
Don't wait.
One hour, one minute, or one second
Could be too late.

Author—The Late William Sanders, Jr. of Union, S.C.

2.   Mama Essie

"Only Memories of Love"

So God has called you home—
Well, Essie Moorehead Sanders (Mama),
How blessed we are to have had you as mother.
God in his infinite wisdom chose us, worthy or not,
as the people here on earth to be exposed most intimately
to your love and kindess, your unending generosity
and your ability to say the words "I love you" so openly and freely.
We have counted on you to always be there.
Sometimes when we were trying to measure up
Sometimes trying to show and tell you how much
we loved and cared for you (in some mighty peculiar ways).
But oh! Oft times using you to share our burdens,
We came to know that these were the times
when you were the loveliest and the best.
We are going to be awfully lonesome Essie.
Lonesome for the gentle touch of your hand and
for the sound of your voice.
Lonesome for the glance of your beautiful face with its
winning smile and of course the disapproving frown when needed.
But we all, Abo (Daddy), Nette, James, and Grady,
know that if we just be still,
you will always be beside us when needed.
It was you, our dearest, who helped us to know God
And how to build and keep our faith in Him
We thank God for giving us an angel (you) for many years.
So long for now our sweet, you've gone home.
We thank God that in due time, we'll meet around His throne.

3. Ode to Brother Grady M.

You, Brother Grady McKinley Sanders, the youngest of the William and Essie Sanders trio—(Marionette 'Nette', James & Grady) were always forging ahead, ready to take a great step or try something new as you glided thru life. So beloved, your "big" brother and "big" sister were not standing near when you took your flight into eternity.

Looking back on the last years of our being together we knew you to be a man at peace with God; whose deepened faith and loving heart had surely prepared you well for your life's final journey. We shall always thank God for you and the memories of the ever charming ways you could make your eyes and facial expressions send a caring and loving "I see you" message across a crowded room.

You most assuredly must now be wrapped tightly in the arms of Jesus. We'll look forward to seeing you when Jesus gathers all "His children" home. Remember you helped us learn to follow love & to know that the ways of love can be hard & steep but the joy and happiness of love overrides its ability to extract pain & suffering.

4.   Ode to Brother James W.

Given all His power and with all His glory, from time to time, softly and ever so gently God grants us a very special blessing or gift. And so it was that those of us who shared a physical-earthly kinship with J. W., Sr. knew that God can and does issue out "special blessings" from time to time.

Those of us who had the privilege to be known as your family long knew you as an Ambassador for Christ. Whenever privileged to be in your presence, we knew that there would be pleasures but also a deepening of spiritual self.

By whatever name of our kinship—wife, child, Daddy, mother, sister, brother, grandpa, grandma, uncle, aunt, cousin or friend, you were ever the teacher, the encourager clothed in a beauty found only in those who are kind, gentle and yet so very strong and learned. My beloved, you possessed a wisdom of life and living which was most assuredly bestowed by God. And yet, in spite of God's mighty presence in your life, you had the capacity to look in awe and with thankfulness at the daily miracles in your life and the life of others.

Brother J.W., you, like Bro. Grady, now know the secrets of life and death which I am yet to learn. You most assuredly must be closer to and perhaps able to commune with the God you loved—unencumbered by the various and mundane interruptions of this world. Dear one your journey here on earth has ended but in the twilight of precious memories, the essence and the meaning of your life will span the distance and *bind* you to us forever.

When we like you come to know the secret of death and approach the gate to eternity, the veil that clouds our eyes now shall be lifted and with hearts and hands outstretched we will speak together again.

5. The Sanders Grandchildren
(Robert, Snooks, Nette, James & Grady)

Like seeds blown in the wind—
Settling side by side in the warm earth for a while—
Each in our own springtime sprouted up.
Growing together—sharing the love of our parents and grandparents—
moving about joyously among the adults—
Never knowing nor always sure of the degree of kinship we were to some
of the adults in our lives. But then no body cared much about that—
Uncle or Aunt to one of us was Uncle or Aunt to all five.

Our job was clear—grow up, he obedient to daddy and mama,
grandpa and grandma, be good children. So we did—each of us carried
by our own breeze and finding our own niche—growing up. Every now
and then, after our teen years our paths would cross and we were again,
the five Sanders children for whatever period of time permitted.

Now, the four of you guys have completed your earthly journey. No
more occasional meetings—no more sharing of fond activities.

But . . . . fond memories there are; memories of your faces and your
voices are as seedlings in a garden after the harvest.

For me, a stranger passes by and there's your walk. Someone talks
or smile and you're there—not as last seen when friends and relatives
comforted me as I mourned your leaving. But in all of the beauty and
fulness of who you were as we lived together in the Garden of life.

No! No! My dear brothers and cousins life experiences bound by
family and mutual love are never lost!

Not even the devilish twinkles or winks of the eyes, the sometime
half grins, the proud stride, your personal pattern presents itself in other
people and you are there!!

First version of this missive was written for cousin Snooks in Nov. 1975.
Revised in 2011 to include memories of cousin Robert and the authors
two Brothers, James & Grady.

IV.

Precious Encounters on the Road of Life

1.   Letter from Rev. William H. Bennett

May 26, 2009

Mrs. Marionette Daniels
St. Mary's Baptist Church
Washington, DC 20012

Dear Sis. Daniels,

This note comes to you just to let you know that there are many people who are praying for you during this season of bereavement. Our hearts are with you as you adjust to life without the physical presence of your beloved husband, Edward. We know that this is often one of the most difficult times in a persons' life and yet we know that you are well acquainted with helping others in their difficult times.

Mrs. Daniels it is exactly because of your having helped so many others through your career and life that we know, God's sweet presence, his precious comforting Holy Spirit has engulfed you and is reassuring you that He will see you through these days and give you bright hope for the tomorrows that He blesses you to have.

My family have been the recipients of your tender loving care for our late father, Rev. William H. Bennett, Sr. and we will never forget the services you helped provide through your program for aging senior citizens which helped them enjoy a more active life even as their time on earth was nearing its' end. We represent hundreds and perhaps even thousands of people who owe you a debt of gratitude for giving of yourself to ensure that our love ones were cared for. We salute your husband for his support of your great works.

There is no way that the God that we serve, will not come to the aid of one like you who has sown so much care into the lives of others, and strengthen you, love you, encourage you and ultimately lift you from this day of weeping and mourning to the bright hope of joy that is yours as you reflect upon how you have seen "the goodness of the Lord in the land of the living." (Psalm 27:13) For Jesus promised in His Sermon on the Mount: "God blesses those who mourn for they shall be comforted." (Matt. 5:4)

So, as the Lord comforts you, I encourage you to use this time to reflect upon the good life that you and your husband enjoyed. I can only imagine with the brilliant mind and quick wit of your husband that you all had some great debates and intellectually stimulating conversations about everything under the sun. Please, go often to your treasure chest of precious memories and think about how in sharing your lives together, God brought you both through the inevitable storms, through every valley, and gave you many mountaintop victories. Through all of this God has used both of you to do a lot of good for many, many people and that is our ultimate purpose on earth, to do good, serve humanity and glorify God by demonstrating His love in our actions.

We say to you and your beloved Edward, thank you for your service to humanity. Thank you for making a wonderful difference in this world. Well done, good and faithful servants!

With eternal gratefulness and love,

Dr. William H. Bennett II
Senior Pastor and Organizer
Good Success Christian Church and Ministries

2. Fifty-two Years of Togetherness (In memory of Essie Moorehead Sanders)

by: William Sanders, Jr.
Union, South Carolina
December, 1978

People who knew looked at us and asked,
"You've been together a long time—How do you get along?"
"Just fine", we would tell them.

Fifty-two years of togetherness, a long time—
Thank God for the memory of them all!

We were alike—but not in all ways,
We did things together—but not everything,
We agreed on many things—but not everything,
We had some of the same talents—but not all,
We had mutual respect—at all times,
We were partners in prayer—every morning.

It wasn't always just the two of us.
Years ago there were three children.
The children—all got married and left.

Then—two lives, one home,
Two people, one family,
One family—born in mutual concern, nourished in respect, blossoming
    in love under the watchful eye of God.

Yes, fifty-two years of togetherness—a long time.
But thank God for them all!

August 8, 2004

3. Moments Remembered for Edward and Marionette Daniels

We offer thanks for the opportunity to contribute to the Daniels' 55th Wedding Anniversary. The Daniels are very dear to me and have been for many years. They were my parents (Eddie and Theressa Clark—both deceased) best friends. My father and Eddie Daniels go back a very long way. I remember them interacting in my home and various other places, as if they were brothers. They laughed, told stories (some of them exaggerated I suspect!) and interacted as if they were practically the same person. And that did not change. Even in more recent years, their relationship was one that just amazed me and (in these later years) my wife. She also came to realize that this was a very special bond. A few years ago, a co-worker of mine (I'm a faculty member at a university), who directs the university's Student Educational Services Center, came up to me and she said "Eddie, I was at a conference and I met this man who asked if I knew you. After I said 'yes', he told me his name and said he was related to you. But I can't recall his name." After some probing of her memory, I realized, with great delight, that she had met Eddie Daniels!!! I was thrilled! I explained to her how close he was to my family, and she said "But I'm sure he said he was related to you". I told her that for all intents and purposes, he was!

My memories of Marionette are incredibly special and I can hardly type this without crying. While I don't recall the details, I do know that when I was very young, perhaps 5 or 6 years old, I played a game called "red light, green light" with her. I suspect that she showed infinite patience in playing with me and I don't think I let her out of my site, since I had finally found someone who was willing to play with me for (what now seems like) hours. It is truly one of my best childhood memories, and I have always been thankful for her attention, joy, smile, and patience. And every time I see her, I remind her of "red light, green light"!! She was one of my mother's best friends and, like the brotherly relationship between Eddie Daniels and my father, seemed more like sisters than friends. I have many wonderful memories of her as a member of the Fashionettes with my mother. When I think of Nette, I realize that "Fashionette" was a perfect name for her!!

I should also mention that Eddie and Nette are my Godparents. As a child, I did not like sitting around listening to the "grown ups" talk. But, I always loved when Ed and Nette came by. There was, and still is, something very special about them.

Finally, I want to note that my wife, Charlesetta (Charley) has come to love them as much as I do. We so much appreciate their calls and cards. She refers to them as "that really jazzy couple"!!! And she says that she hopes we are like them when we get older!

I could go on, but I will stop here. God has truly blessed us by putting Ed and Nette in our lives. I literally have to keep myself from crying every time I hear from them—they mean that much to me, and now to my wife also.

Ed and Nette: Congratulations on your 55th Wedding Anniversary and thank you for being in our lives. God Bless you both!!

Love,

Eddie and Charlesetta Clark

August 25, 2001

4.   Just a Tribute

TO: EDWARD AND MARIONETTE DANIELS
             In Recognition of their Enduring
             and Inspiring Relationship.

FROM: The Whitehurst Family: Bill, Patsy, Angelyn, Donna
                                       William III, Arlene and Joyce.

To cast our friendship in a time perspective, we have to travel back
to the years 1946 and 1947. The place was West Virginia State College
(now University) in Institute, West Virginia. This was the arena in which
Bill first met these two truly outstanding human beings and began a
friendship, brotherhood, sisterhood which prevails until this very day.

Our paths crossed again in Washington, D.C. The year was 1951.
For a short while we were practically neighbors, living only three to four
blocks from each other. Small World Isn't It? Several dynamics transpired
during this time. We were in graduate school at American and Howard
Universities: Bill and Patsy began to add to the population, ultimately
reaching the magic number of five offsprings. Ed and Nette adopted all of
the kids and have remained in their corner throughout the years.

In addition to the pursuit of educational excellence at the graduate
school level, we were embroiled in keeping the home fires burning
through adequate employment. Bill recalls working with Ed at the
Maryland Children' Center in Catonsville. As a matter of fact, Bills car
deserted him and at one point in time Ed let him use his sports roadster
for nearly a month or more. Such consideration and friendship can never
be repaid.

However, this does not end the story. Ed and Nette moved to New
York City where Ed continued his work with delinquent teen-agers and
Nette in the Social Services area. They arranged for me to visit at least
two innovative programs involved in identifying and serving school-age
youth who were unable to use their school experience profitably. Bill was
working with the D. C. Public School System as Supervising Director of
the Child and Youth Study Division. These exposures were invaluable

in helping develop new approaches for the D.C. School program. We continued to maintain contact throughout the New York City Years.

Ed and Nette moved back to D.C. in the late 1970's, I believe. Prior to the permanent relocation, Ed served as a consultant to a municipal department in D.C. and worked with Bill in the area of planning. His services proved to be of inestimable value. Later Ed became a full-time staff member. Ed and Bill's work relationship continued into the post retirement period. Both were involved with several contractual enterprises with individuals identified as health care leaders in the District of Columbia.

The recapitulation of the history of the Daniels-Whitehurst Saga could go on and on. There is so much more to relate. Hopefully, the above information will provide you with a "birds-eye-view" of a friendship that has spanned the years.

We pray God's Blessings on these two very special individuals who, through their compassion, love, friendship, concern and dedication to the uplift of humanity, both broadly and specifically, have earned the admiration and respect of all.

The Whitehursts
Bill, Patsy and Children

P.S. Take written mistake for hugs & kisses.

5.   It Only Takes a Moment

October 11, 2011

Hello Mrs. Daniels,

I was thinking about you. So—I decided to write a letter of acknowledgment I wanted to share a bit of myself with you.

The last time we spoke I expressed some of my daily life concerns, to you. And in return you always give me words of encouragement and spiritual guidance. Eventhough our time was brief and in passing. Just the nature of the conversation is so powerful (You always make me tear up.) You remind me of my grandmother a very sweet, classy and admiring lady. All the things I'd like to be. Your words come from experience, knowledge and just a genuine care I wish more people were like you. Thank you Mrs. Daniels, for everything.

P.S. See you soon!

Sincerely,
—K. Cameron
2011

6. Precious Moments Bursting Forth

August 20, 2004

To all the nieces and nephews of Uncle Ed and Aunt Nette,

It may be a surprise for you to know that you have some "cousins" living down in Mexico. Even more surprising is that these cousins consist of a Cameroonian and a New York Jew. Add to that the fact that Uncle Ed and Aunt Nette's grand nephew (six and a half years old) says that he is half African, half New York, and half Mexican! For most that might be hard to take, but Uncle Ed and Aunt Nette will take it all in stride.

Having no biological aunts or uncles, it may seem natural that in my early childhood years I would quickly adopt Uncle Ed and Aunt Nette to play those roles. But even if I had biological "tios" and "tias," I doubt that they could have supplanted these two wonderful human beings in this part of my life.

My earliest memories of Uncle Ed go back to when he and my Dad worked together at the juvenile delinquent center in Maryland. It was a time when the beat generation was making its mark and many of my schoolmates wanted to emulate that "cool" style. There was Uncle Ed with his sports cap and MG coupe—it would be hard to imagine a more dapper or more "cool," fellow. But that was just the surface stuff. Uncle Ed provided an example for me of a sensitive, thoughtful, intelligent but strong, role model. The fact that he cared so much about people, and worked hard on their behalf, probably rubbed off on me as well.

Aunt Nette—well she struck me as one eloquent and elegant woman—not to mention darn good looking! Our discussions over the years, due to my absence from the country, have been too few, but they have always been thought-provoking and have come from someone with a very big heart. This has been further expressed in her poetry—which gets even better when one hears it from her own lips. Oh yea, she is still one darn good-looking woman!

These might sound like the reflections of a friend, but many years ago when our family went through a crisis when my younger brother was hit and nearly killed by a car, it was Uncle Ed who came to our house and provided a sense of calm reassurance to us kids while my mother and father spent literally days at the hospital. On a lighter note, Uncle Ed also dealt with the crisis of my old Nissan pick-up truck with a leaky gas line—but you'll have to ask him about that for the details. Try not to get him laughing too hard!

The warm connection my family and I have had, and continue to have and feel for Uncle Ed and Aunt Nette goes back to formative years and is entwined with memories of my father and life in Maryland and later New York. When we do manage to get together, Uncle Ed, Aunt Nette, and I always manage to talk about social and political issues and events and how they affect our lives and have changed (or not changed) over the decades. Those talks are always a real treat too and I reflect upon them as yet another special connection to this very special couple. Finally, we talk about old times and people and places we have known together—as might be expected when family gets together.

We regret that we cannot be there with the rest of the nieces and nephews to help celebrate this wedding anniversary "through the years" with Uncle Ed and Aunt Nette, but please know that our thoughts and hearts are with you on this occasion that allows us all to cherish this beautiful people.

Love,

Paul & Grace Poland

7. Precious Memories Continued

Dear Aunt Nette and Uncle Ed,

I am sending you love and my deepest apology for not being able to attend the celebration of your 55th anniversary. I know this is a joyous occasion for you both, and I know you are surrounded by many love ones, family, and friends.

I really wanted to be a part of your celebration and recall some of the fond memories I have of you.

Uncle Ed, I remember many years ago when I was a little girl you came to Virginia to spend some time with Nan and Papa and you and I made a grove. You and I cleaned out this wooded area and made some crude benches out of scrap pieces of wood. I remember you telling me we had to find some large rocks, but they had to have a certain sheen, because once we placed them, the rain would wash them and the sun would make them pretty and white. The conversation we had in that grove is lost in time, but I remember us sitting there, me with my legs dangling, and just enjoying what we had made. Even after you had left, there were still many days I enjoyed sitting alone in that grove.

Aunt Nette, I remember you always smelled so nice and you always gave us kisses and left your lipstick on our faces. Please understand that is not a complaint. You openly showed your love for us in your own special way. I also remember the pajamas you use to give us. Of course, being kids, we always preferred a toy, but we sure were glad to snuggle into those pajamas on those cold winter nights.

. . . . and to this day, I still talk about the week I spent in New York with you both. You introduced me to fine dining, Broadway plays, and Macy's!!!! Thank you both for the memories.

Happy 55th Anniversary and I hope you both continue to be blessed.

Much love,
Your niece

Gail

8/2004

V.
The End

1.   Through the Years with Uncle Ed and Aunt Nette

Through the years with Ed and Nette Daniels as they made their way through 60 years (1949-2009) sharing a love of God, family and people underpinned by love and a great passion for each other.

Uncle Ed and Aunt Nette thru the years.

1949

1961

1974

2004

2009

2. Note to the Reader

Beloved, I sincerely hope your journey through this missive has been enjoyable, inspiring and whatever else one might find helpful as you go through the journey of life. You have now shared the life of this ole lady whose pathway was filled with so many beautiful human beings. Best of all? God allowed me to meet, court, marry and live with Eddie Daniels for 60 years, during which time we shared an unyielding passion and love for each other. Let the love of Christ abide in your heart from this moment on.

Love You,
Aunt Nette

Edwards Brothers Malloy
Oxnard, CA USA
September 13, 2013